FINISHING LINE PRESS

www.finishinglinepress.com

my imaginary old man: poems

poems by

Ryan Sharp

Finishing Line Press
Georgetown, Kentucky

my imaginary old man: poems

ACKNOWLEDGMENTS

Berkley Poetry Review: [in dreams there is still the dream that he was]; [the red
oak broken the yellow lawn broke]
DIALOGIST: [this is a good place to begin from here]
JAAM: [my imaginary old man says his three] (published as "the enigma of my
imaginary old man"); [the unsown stories the blackened pictures] (published as
"the imaginary old man")
Silk Road: [my imaginary old man sits makes tea] (published as "birch branches
and my imaginary old man"); [my imaginary old man is a blind man] (published
as "The tiny chasm of my imaginary old man")
The Ilanot Review: [everyone knows what kind of man he is] ; [to see my
imaginary old man]; [most all was taken from him his home his]

Publisher: Leah Maines

Editor: Christen Kincaid

Cover Art: Ryan Sharp

Author Photo: Abigail Sharp

Cover Design: Elizabeth Maines

Author inquiries and mail orders:
Finishing Line Press
P. O. Box 1626
Georgetown, Kentucky 40324
U. S. A.

Table of Contents

Table of Contents

this is a good place to begin from here
my imaginary old man appears
something beginning here in the event
beginning is such a thing for the old
man the doorway is a beginning the wood
porch and peeled paint the uneven rotted
steps the drive leading to the road rumbling
over the bridge following the river
past hills leaning into where the big sky
begins surely there is a beginning
something is perceived first as a shadow
then a bear then a small child then bear
the sky is perceived as the ocean then
a small redness
         all that begins does so
in many ways which is to say that there
is no end to it which is to say that
when nothing happens he waits for it to
begin whatever it is that is beginning
we are getting closer some light falling
some hinge some door closing softly as if
for forever and again forever

most all was taken from him his home his
children the garden even existence
people say somebody maybe his own
old man made my imaginary old
man but others like to think we create
ourselves as ourselves maybe it was me
who made him from what sticks and mud stones song
memory anything i could scrape
                                        up i
have built a tree here i told it to grow
there like him in so many words i put
it next to the house and inside i placed
him a while until he was not i
carved a river back the house where he was
for those bright times he was a bridge over
the water where he could read might bathe there
a hill i grew overlooks the setting
i set him in the place i made sticks
mud stones song memory every
                                        piece i made

a thought comes to me here that he may have
made me make it this way or it was made
through me in some way the tree is for me
so i might know what he looks like a tree

to see my imaginary old man
one must first see parts all the moving gears
spent oil and straw fingernails the grime
beneath worn eyelids hinge jaw feathering
the neck bone to see him really see him
whole you must not blink let the eyes blur deep
into the voice burning rubber to catch
what loose gravel churns in his tired throat
let your small drums steal all the timbre then
only then will edges slow cut away
from shadow will the cleft emerge bridging
the cauliflower ears to grease the lens
make it sugar soft would be dishonest
he is more than that than what catches light
than what can be held or tied to a tree
you have to see him hard that way you see
him skin and stubble wings
                              you cannot see
the whole butterfly before you know it
beyond its parts first you see only wings
then proboscis then eye and legs amen
only once the butterfly gets its name
does it become real the naming itself
pulling together fragile pieces name
blessing the butterfly whole in a word
amen the word being frail beginning
amen
          he always says it is better
to look at everything sideways to see
it blurring from the dark periphery

everything approached from the front will flee
the trick is to circle in to draw close
as if by accident see it before
it sees you looking to hold it before
it knows it is pressed flat a butterfly

the unsown stories the blackened pictures
the closet man the thing escaping sight
the wearer of grandmother pajamas
the under the bed monster the sleepy
wet eyes like doorknobs the old smell elbows
worn razor sharp the hands that give away
the age the cold armchair the feet that ran
the farthest the dancing shoes the vacant
wooden frame the man who appears in the
mirror when the name is recanted three
times the weekend catcher the image one
creates to fill the heart shaped hole the fool
gold the shine in the oil slick the sick
lion the most cunning the fox
the highest sour grape the trophy hawk
the bear clawed the beehive of things the honey
comb words the words shaped like prisms that shine
or are sullied by the angle the barbed
words the parts of the elephant the blind
men cannot find with their thick hands thinly
boiled fictions the sunny side up truths
the santa suit that was too large to fill
the cherubim that never really looked
like a baby the prodigal old man
the push broom upper lip the sandpaper
jowls the whiteout smile the arms big enough
to hold more the dim hand in the pocket
the river pushing the big stones deeper

*

the encroaching shadow of the shrinking
forest the foreshadowed shadow the storm
before and after the storm the quiet
outside of the quiet the chaos inside the quiet
room the room that is no longer a room

i am these poems
in so many words they are
my bones skin and all the custard

in dreams there is still the dream where he was
different everything was the tree bent
its shadow toward the road not the river
the lilies pushing up the hill into
a mountain hold their tongues the blind flowers
each lying upon each each needing each
no rough hand filching what few white petals
how the bridge did not shake here the temple
is made out of breath not mud and bricks
he remembers there being a child
somewhere off in his periphery but
that is as far as it goes the dreaming
that is still the waking and the living

my imaginary old man is here
despite what they say here he knows he is
here even the unreal get their own song
the unreal still fill at least their own song
have worn like an old tree in several
directions at once have drawn into the night
as the tree wears he draws into the night
as the song dies behind the tree
                                    he says
if i stay here long trouble will find me
he says if i stay i may never leave
i want to hold time still like stone i want
to hold it down and breathe its feathers in
my imaginary old man himself
a bird like time his arms held out flying
i follow him a bird our mouths knives our
hands cupping air wings casting long shadows
they seem to mean something but they do not
they are only our bird shadows which seem
enough or not enough if i go now
he says there might still be time to forget
soon it will be time to leave but to where
he is always leaving somewhere always
he made me how i am he made me who
if one counts time we are three birds in one

is flint to stone tool to twig feathering
fire is full of five different types of wont
and want is everywhere now but only
sometimes is skin past flesh to bone and time
is flecks of bright gold stitched into dried mud
flat is seeds wishing is please in the dark
is not dream and dream is not what was said
but also is every word of it is
butterfly old light and cave is often
listening meaning silent is trying
to regain control of his own image
is both water warping and drinking straw
is exit wounds and theme park churro is
steeped in part truth and part pure cane sugar
is complicated is space between wing
and church is split seams and bridges falling
down is odd flight but intentional is
white dress shirt and spilt wine is home but far
from it is new song but old words i know

my imaginary old man is a blind man alone in the movie theater he sees without seeing he feels what cannot be seen he can tell what is said and what is not said what is screamed the sound of screeching tires gasps he keeps his box of milk duds in the seat next to him he rests his muddy boots on the headrest below him there are those parts of the movie that are without sound a hollow gulley they are the hardest for my imaginary old man forgets where he is a tiny chasm he could be anywhere in those seconds home in his den in his old armchair as if he can see everything again he does not wish to see

last night he dreamt
bougainvillea spilled over
his head like a tsunami

the red oak broken the yellow lawn broke
the old red brick house broken juiced for all
its copper the red door broken his room
breaks off the end of the hallway he broke
his armchair broke his hands broken shovels
his shoulders break downward his voice breaks
a broken pipeline his two ears broken
torches his eyes crushed white calla lilies
broken he says history is something
else his words torn lemons his broken
burden the scratched records his children
broken songbirds his wives string and paper
                                                                cups

my imaginary old man carries
a battered suitcase of blackening moths
and broken watches white tube socks to feed
the moths he cares too much for the almost
butterflies like most he sees himself in
winged things small odes to wind and revival
to be reborn bright and beautiful like
a butterfly that is one of his dreams
like most though he is more like his moths how
they pepper to shadow the pollutants

before the fall he had all the makings
of an activist his wide owl eyes
his silver bullet tongue all his untamed
salt and pepper facial hair he had spun
years of cotton into then he could have
marched a whole kingdom of moths across
the riverbed the way he would have held
his long fingers out in front of the crowd
like constellations he has always been
skilled at the performance of dying but
not staying dead
                            after his first death all
that was left behind was dust light matter
a suit worn thin in the knees and pockets
deep in depression deep as a dirt grave
he never named anything he could not
bury he is practiced at digging holes
at deep turning the feel of wet soil
sifting through his deep space hands we know him
for his vastness goes on for good even
in his most illusory moments
the soot stained moths that could be trees like his
whole hands realized in the milky way mud
feeling for root or stone to turn over
stars that go on for forever like him

my imaginary old man himself
an archive having already cornered
the market on utterance meaning he
keeps memory on a tight lease meaning this
is as he wishes meaning he cannot
help himself even for him ideas are
constructed within the constraints of what
can be imagined when his eyes are closed
three old men who have yet to be appear
seated around a candle lit bare chest
to chin by thin fire small black pools tucked
inside the cradles of their collarbones
the dark outside of the old men beneath
his eyelids vaster for the candle and
them defining the dark big the darkness
too a plinth the old men have yet to leave

that imaginary old man could sing
hymns all day with his eyes closed his upturned
palms testing the stale canary yellow
air for the perfume of broken songbirds
blue notes trembling out of tired throats
they can live again in his riverbed
hands his slow curling fingers lazarus
plants killing themselves a little to live

the old bell his throat
cracked clang sang out a blue note
the boned tone moment bone dry

inside my imaginary old man
lies the imaginary old man that
came before him and inside the old man
that came before my imaginary
old man lies another and inside him
another and so on it goes   old men

all the way down

the memory cannot contain everything
the sounds sounding the broken getting broke
some heal each flicker of light some sparks sieve
the river filling and letting loose trees
combing through big sky further off fires
burning we know those times when we can
not grab all of the falling leaves the shrapnel
smoke and blast that second that everything
that grows in the acorn the staggering
spiral promising to be back sooner
or later he says i am not the knot
to be untied he says it is woven
into my thread
                      somewhere there is the song
of the joker the sad clown mirror you
do not need a mirror to see what is
this fire is all there is left to find
the mirror a broken chair a symbol

my imaginary old man sits makes tea begins whittling small wives out of birch branches with the blade he keeps buried beneath his rock hard pillow he carves them with no hands no mouths teeth he carves them baby making hips shaped like question marks the small wives have no idea of the imaginary lives set ahead of them the casseroles gone cold the phantom phone calls the wilted transparent flowers he already knows how he will say he is sorry how he will explain that he is a man who is not really there he carves the small wives from memory one smokes virginia slims painted red another he calls mary he carves with abandon all the white grain curled on the packed dirt floor he soon sees the dozen or so he has carved are not enough he whittles more until the wood is not enough he creates branches with his words that are not enough he storms out his tea has been cold for years

the hero of his own time a small ship
handbuilt inside the now broken bottle
the green go for broke sunday suit the silk
tongued the confused form the smoke blown over
the angry bees the dark heat born into
the chiaroscuro painting the black
derby on the pavement the lemon juice
love letter the most baroque the talents
buried under the bougainvillea
the scythe sliding through green grain the gloved
hand holding the candlestick the trembling
pillar of salt the living ghost the light
bending the twig in the glass of water
the lost sheep the knowledge contained within
the apple seed the owl necked the bird
held up in the bush the deliberate
old enigma the handsome tar baby
the genius child the brer rabbit
of libras the basquiat of tumble
weeds the lonesome falling tree full of sound

*

the tree the fruit fell from the abandoned
garden the obsolete fig leaves the grain
of the split white wood the turned over stone

i saw say i saw
believe what i saw saw me
believing i say i saw

my imaginary old man says that
his three bellybuttons are just that not
old bullet holes he caught in iowa
an enigma in baltimore he lived
so close to washington but nowhere near
he says his feet itch something terrible
from time to time he calls and asks about
the mariners i say the whole ocean
is full these days but mostly i am not
that sure he knows who i am at this age
no one sees him my imaginary
old man does not come around too often
he dines and dashes
                              they say he has bird
bones but who believes that i remember
saturdays mostly he had his christmas
tree up all year i remember how his
day old shaved face felt like a gravel road

my imaginary old man has it
hard all the poems of his absence no
song sings of his burden how he never knows
how to hold his babies he is known for
sleeping the quiet required after
his imaginary work the silent
threat he represents no one ever thanks
him after touchdowns or being handed
an award only when he became so

old and fragile did he earn empathy
when he was too small to do too much harm
being somewhere something one could never
touch being unreal was his greatest gift

he says in his dream he drowns the lovely
white women troubling the surface water
above his glowing head his shimmering
children becoming like him jellyfish

after the house was repainted that blue
that bleed like a vein into the river
he could not find his way home for many
years I sat squinting the stoop pulling
away from foundation oiling my glove
until like nothing he showed up folded
arms behind him scaled wings new wet edges
softened by dusk old light saying he had
a present saying he had changed again

my imaginary old man could have
been a minister before one of his
wives packed the minivan during his day
shift he says often it is easier
not to be right i say i believe in
a few things it is what it is he says
he never knows what day it is the man
never really needs to be anywhere
but home he says that would be nice i say

in my last dream my imaginary
old man holds out his hand to me i think
i take it but who ever really knows
the old day doesn't bring light like it should
the wet grass stays damp under the lawn chairs
singing in the rain the old man holds still
he sings so i sing his eyes close my eyes
close our wide open mouths catching fire

all i ever did
he says was paint bright sunlight
on the side of the blue house

Born in Spokane, WA, **Ryan Sharp** spent most of his youth bouncing around the Pacific Northwest before his family set roots in Portland, OR. There he received his MFA in Writing from Pacific University while teaching English at a charter high school outside of Portland. Currently living in Austin, TX with his beautiful wife, Abigail, and two children, Judah and Eden, he is a PhD candidate in the English Department at the University of Texas at Austin where his research focuses on contemporary Black American persona poetry and how it is being employed to resist and revise archival representations of Blackness.

He also teaches and serves as the Writers' Studio Coordinator at Huston-Tillotson University, a Historically Black University in East Austin. His poetry and reviews have appeared in several journals including *Berkeley Poetry Review, Callaloo, Copper Nickel, DIALOGIST,* and *PANK.* He has been the editor of *Borderlands: Texas Poetry Review* since 2013.

www.ingramcontent.com/pod-product-compliance
Lightning Source LLC
LaVergne TN
LVHW021126080426
835510LV00021B/3343